Rational Numbers

RATIONAL NUMBERS

POEMS BY H. L. HIX

For Nancy:

"What is finite to the understanding
is nothing to the heart." —Feuerbach

Copyright © 2000 Truman State University Press
All rights reserved
www2.truman.edu/tsup

Printed by Thomson-Shore, Dexter, Michigan, USA

Cover illustration: "...paradise so far" by Jim Sajovic, Kansas City Art Institute
Cover design: Teresa Wheeler, Truman State University designer

Body type ITC Legacy Serif 11/13. Display type ITC Legacy Serif 13/13.

Library of Congress Cataloging-in-Publication Data (Applied For)

   Hix, H. L.
      Rational numbers: poems / H. L. Hix.
      p. cm.
      ISBN 0-943549-80-9 (alk. paper)
      ISBN 0-943549-79-5 (pbk.: alk. paper)

The paper in this publication meets or exceeds the minimum requirements of the
American National Standard—Permanence of Paper for Printed Library Materials,
ANSI Z39.48 (1984).

I dedicate certain decimals of "Orders of Magnitude"
to particular individuals:

"Water searching for itself…" to Loren Graham

"I used to canoe…" to David and Bethany Daniel

"Three hundred years…" to Sheri and J. Helt

"Look at the person…" to Hal Wert

"I have seen her…" to Sheila

"From frozen tarn…" to Steve Cromwell

"Hope names its own…" to the memory of Roy Helt

"In the new world…" to Sheila

"I make it my principle…" to Sheila

"Centaurea Cyanus…" to Jüri Talvet

"Cat with no collar…" to Naomi Shihab Nye

"Airfield first…" to Clyde Badger

"Next to my favorite…" to Jan Zwicky

"How could I taste…" to Sheila

"How do you like paradise…" to the Hal and Tinsley Wert family

"Friends feel pain…" to Tautvyda Marcinkevičiūtė

CONTENTS

Acknowledgments ix

Attributions xi

Orders of Magnitude 1

Figures 39

ACKNOWLEDGMENTS

I am grateful to the editors of the following magazines, in whose pages portions of these poems first appeared: *Chattahoochee Review, Cider Press Review, Delmar, Denver Quarterly, Forpoetry.com, Green Mountains Review, Janus, Laurel Review, New Letters, Northwest Review, Permafrost, Phoebe, Poem, Poet Lore, The Review, Tundra, Widener Review,* and *Writers' Forum.*

The stichomythic sections from "Figures" were first published in the anthology *Poets at Large* 1996 (Helicon Nine Editions).

"Go and look behind the altar" was included in *The Hand of the Poet,* an exhibition curated by Rodney Phillips and held at the New York Public Library, and in *Poems for the New Century,* a limited-edition portfolio produced in conjunction with that exhibition.

A selection of decimals from "Orders of Magnitude" was included in *Intellectual Pleasures,* a limited edition by Aralia Press. I thank Michael Peich and his fellow artisans for their painstaking work and for the beautiful volume that resulted from it.

Other decimals from "Orders of Magnitude" enjoy a second life in the visual work of artists Kyoung Ae Cho, Anne Lindberg, Judi Ross, and Piper Shepard, including presentation in a limited edition by Judi Ross, *This Translucent Tissue.* I thank these four outstanding artists for seeing the poems as beeswax and feathers, as wood and silk and their own hair.

I thank Joseph Duemer and Rush Rankin for critical responses to earlier drafts of this book.

ATTRIBUTIONS

The epigraphs come from the following sources, in order of their appearance: Borislav Pekič, *The Time of Miracles*; Jan Zwicky, *Songs for Relinquishing the Earth*; Michael J. Duff, "The Theory Formerly Known as Strings"; Jean-Jacques Rousseau, *On Social Contract*; Paul Bowles, *The Sheltering Sky*; Marianne Boruch, *Poetry's Old Air*.

Seven of the decimals in "Orders of Magnitude" respond to works of visual art by these current or former colleagues at Kansas City Art Institute: Kyoung Ae Cho, Kristine Diekman, William Easton, Anne Lindberg, Karen McCoy, Judi Ross, Piper Shepard.

One responds to the description of model 761 in the Ware Collection of Glass Flowers and Fruit, Harvard Museum.

Each remaining decimal incorporates a (sometimes manipulated) fragment of text from another source. For several, that source text is an African-American spiritual. The other sources are: Aristotle, *Nicomachean Ethics*; Artemidorus, *The Interpretation of Dreams*; Augustine, *On Christian Doctrine*; Jean Baudrillard, *Fatal Strategies, Seduction*; William Blake, *The Four Zoas*, letter to William Hayley, *The Marriage of Heaven and Hell*, *Visions of the Daughters of Albion*; Marianne Boruch, *Poetry's Old Air*; Albert Camus, *The Myth of Sisyphus, The Rebel*; William Benton Clulow, *Aphorisms and Reflections*; Nicholas Cusanus, *The Layman: About Mind, On Learned Ignorance, On Peaceful Unity of Faith, A Scrutiny of the Koran*; Hester Chapone, *Letters on the Improvement of the Mind*; Leopold Damrosch, Jr., *Symbol and Truth in Blake's Myth*; René Descartes, *The Passions of the Soul*; Denis Diderot, *Jacques the Fatalist*; Umberto Eco, *Six Walks in the Fictional Woods*; James Elkins, *The Poetics of Perspective*; Maud Ellmann, *The Hunger Artists*; Eliza Ware Farrar, *The Young Lady's Friend*; Susan L. Feagin, *Reading with Feeling*; Sigmund Freud, *The Interpretation of Dreams, Introductory Lectures*; William Gass, *On Being Blue*; Louise Glück, *Proofs and Theories*; Johann Wolfgang Goethe, *Theory of Colours*; Donald Hall, *Life Work*; C. L. Hardin, *Color for Philosophers*; Václav Havel, *Open Letters*; Thomas Hobbes, *Leviathan*; Immanuel Kant, *Groundwork of the Metaphysics of Morals*; Søren Kierkegaard, *Philosophical Fragments, The Sickness Unto Death*; Julia Kristeva, *Desire in Language*; Lao-Tzu, *Tao te Ching*; Walter Lowrie, *A Short Life of Kierkegaard*; Georg Lukács, *The Theory of the Novel*; Jean-François Lyotard, *The Differend, Libidinal Economy*; Karl Marx, *The German Ideology*; W. S. Merwin, letter to Harry Ford; John Stuart Mill, *The Subjection of Women*; Richard Edouard Moritz, *Memorabilia Mathematica*; Toni Morrison, *Beloved*; Iris Murdoch, *The Sovereignty of Good*; Friedrich Nietzsche, *The Gay Science, Will to Power*; Robert Nozick, *The Nature of Rationality*; Nicole Oresme, *Treatise on the Geometry of Qualities and Motions*; Plotinus, *Enneads*; Antonio Porchia, *Voices*; Jean-Jacques Rousseau, *Confessions, Discourse on Inequality, Emile, On Social Contract, Reveries of the Solitary Walker*; Bertrand Russell, *Intro-*

duction to Mathematical Philosophy, *The Philosophy of Mathematics*; Elaine Scarry, *Resisting Representation*; Amartya Sen, *Poverty and Famines*; Debra Spark, "Last Things"; Susan Rubin Suleiman, *Risking Who One Is*; Emmanuel Swedenborg, *The Divine Love and the Divine Wisdom*; Marina Tsvetaeva, *Art in the Light of Conscience*; Gregory Ulmer, *Applied Grammatology*; Luisa Valenzuela, *Bedside Manners*; Eudora Welty, *One Writer's Beginnings*; Ludwig Wittgenstein, *Philosophical Investigations*; Jan Zwicky, *Lyric Philosophy*.

...mathematics was an elegy.

What is truth when I'm dying?

Orders of Magnitude

For decades, physicists have been struggling to understand nature at
the extremely small scales near the Planck length of 10^{-33} centimeter.
We have always supposed that laws of nature, as we know them,
break down at smaller distances. What T-duality suggests,
however, is that at these scales, the universe looks just
the same as it does at large scales. One may even
imagine that if the universe were to shrink to less
than the Planck length, it would transform
into a dual universe that grows bigger as
the original one collapses.

Moral quantities cannot be expressed with mathematical precision.

Here begins the work of darkness in which
I've been encrypted these ten pent terms past,
the tome of tombs, script of skulls, the lie
I leave in lieu of a life. Here begins
my negative, in which all corneas
are black, all pupils and irises white,
in which you are darkness, damn you. Let this
be fair warning, let it loose a lesson,
but let it not pretend truth. Here begins
the work of darkness in whose lap I lie.

•

I subscribe neither to species nor sex.
Weightless, I lean not into wind or wall.
I hear sniper fire in Sarajevo
but never claw my shattered shin as if
to pull out the pain. I ride through riots
in LA but am not dragged from my rig
to read and reread iron. The short ride
from *Honey hand me my pants* to *I have
to do what's right for me* I know because
friends call when they arrive. These are their words.

•

Everything takes on a new appearance
after your daughter has drowned. Think yourself
into this: school trip to the lake, you're late
to her carpool, say *Hurry!* but forget
to kiss her goodbye, no one notices
when she goes under, a diver searching
for coins finds her face down on the bottom.
Everything takes on a greenish-brown tint.
Every step, your feet find mud and algae.
Water tests everything now, and all gold sinks.

•

3

Shocking disasters lie deeply hidden
in comforting numbers. Bodies surface
downstream, flesh pale as fish. Dogs sniff out their
scattered limbs. Boys find them under bridges.
Shocking lies hide deeply. Famine favors
foreigners. Humans die in comforting
numbers. A dog eating a corpse begins
with the brain. Promise. Disasters surface
downstream: scattered limbs, lies, corpses of fish.
Hidden shocks favor humans. Breathe deeply.

•

Water searching for itself under rocks.
Rocks rounding into light under water.
Trout twinned with water, with stones streamed slick.
So many guilelessnesses sprung from such
a sire, a god by the name of chaos,
so many songs sung to the human eye.
First rocks become trout and trout become light,
then light becomes water and water song.
Last, the human eye can hear god wading
across trout-slick stones, searching for himself.

•

Go and look behind the altar. My god,
my broken god, cowers there a-weeping.
Tears and drool mingle in his rheum-stained beard.
Tiny ash-fragile angels worship him,
singing a song of melting cellophane,
sizzle of ice crystals singed off a log,
snap of burning sap. Look behind my god;
look through him. Skin brittle as burned paper.
He weeps not for his own long withering
but for my short solo, sung sans seraph.

•

It's not the satin-lined coffin I mind,
but the store-bought sympathy card before.
Not stopped heart, flat EEG, dry mirror,
but testicular cancer, breast cancer,
colon cancer, chemo with its baldness
and retching, the incisions, excisions,
decisions, the futile hard-on that marks
the moment of death. Sponge baths, cold bedpans,
latex gloves. Not having to leave this world,
but having to bow so low to do it.

•

The cat that killed the cardinal chick needs
the nourishment to care for its kittens.
Long live reproduction, long live hungry
mouths, the boy who beats up his brother for
the last ice cream bar, the brother who gets
beaten up but whom hunger educates.
Let there be always more of us: eating
each other means we are not dying from
emphysema or meningitis. May
the parent birds live to lay next year's egg.

•

The time of the earthquake. The character
of the crime. *You piece of shit.* Words to sing
on the way to school. Words to remember.
Words to live by. *You. piece. of. shit.* Help comes
after earthquakes and crimes. One day's whiskers.
One day's tears. And the fourth generation.
This will teach you to lie to me again.
In time for the earthquake. In time to sing.
You piece of shit. The brutal, spellbinding
honesty of honest brutality.

•

I used to canoe across the tidal
marshes to the mouth of hell. On nest stands
tall as gallows ospreys stretched their strong wings.
Warning. An osprey's one expression says
No forgiveness. An osprey's gaze insists
god sees us through hunters' eyes. The currents
here in strong tides will take you out to sea.
Gutted by gulls, crabshells litter the point.
I used to row right through the rushes past
ospreys to the mouth of hell. And go in.

•

I first found blackberries more dangerous
than nipples, more pernicious to bared flesh
than hornets' nests, when a low cloud caught me
climbing Ragged before dawn. I wanted
to see sunrise from the summit, the long
spine of the other hills, a hawk circling
below me. I wanted to see the coast,
the next range, another land, but I saw
the cloud and I stopped for the blackberries
that stained me with their juice and my own blood.

•

Spring sang saturated roses sinking
under superfluity, bent down by
embarrassing abundance, but summer
lurched in today like lightning, sudden heat
effecting revelation: what was lost
found by the flash, fetched from sodden shadows.
Late but swarming like locusts, the extreme
temperature of transubstantiation
suffocates our bodies that beckoned it,
begging to become, impossibly, god.

•

To prove god moves on the wings of the wind,
how many hawks watching from how many
road signs, fenceposts, treetops? How red their wings
when at rest, how white in flight? How many
mice must die, how beautifully, to feed
their wheeling? How many Canada geese
clattering from how many stubble fields,
their panicked rising from the horizon
thunderhead dark, need to settle onto
this frozen lake to show the angels fell?

•

When angels fall in love, whole new hells form.
The explosion flashes across the sky.
In classrooms the wide universe over
children weep, inconsolable, branded
by the flames, eyes shielded from the plunging
parabola of smoke. Rubble plummets
to the sea. After deaths that send out light
no bodies surface. The other angels
still imitate galaxies in clustered
praise, but their songs ever after are lies.

•

I set god free from the owl that waited
too late and rose too slow. Next afternoon
from the pronghorn that tried to stop but slid
across wet asphalt in front of my truck.
Now god speaks again, from the pendulum
tracing earth's arc in sand, from the rhythmic
rap-rapping of the roofer's air hammer,
from the squeals of girls on a trampoline.
I set god free to speak to me again.
I no longer understand, but I hear.

•

God's two wills, *Screen Door Banging in the Wind*
and *Melting Snow Sliding off a Windshield*,
will learn how to hear each other across
seasons and unlikeness. Got to kill. Turn
now: this wind means more banging. No slow snow
sloping down will shield you. Wait for more heat.
God, you still mean screen door, t-shirt, low rent,
earn our roof the wrong way, sweat stains, sweet shame
the color of blood. I will get you back.
Got to know how. God, too, will learn to bow.

·

I am accustomed to contests: my first
tug-of-war was to the death. Tightening
the nurse-noose around my neck, mother tried
at every contraction to strangle me.
I tried to eviscerate her with that
very vein, and did. So I'll die later,
more slowly, in the infernal method,
by corrosives: father's lifelong failure
to forgive, infrequent but vivid dreams,
distrust of songbirds. The one real contest.

·

The thought of death is my dancing partner,
a fine one. She laughs too much, but we whirl,
I a fallen leaf, she the wind. Stars swirl,
a mirrored ball, such fiery tesserae.
The thought of dancing with my fine partner
is death, but she won't let me sit. I've drunk
too much. She swirls like the night sky. Sweat beads
light her fine, fiery face. I've swirled too much.
She says she wants me. She's drunk. I'm dizzy.
The thought of dancing with my death is fine.

·

Three hundred years leaves little legible.
The dates of mothers dead at twenty-five
beside their daughters dead at nine. Winged skulls,
winged cherubs, winged portraits. Nothing but blurs
on marble or sandstone, which last hardly
longer than we. Granite fractures and slate
segments. Stones sink and slant. Neither risen
nor fallen know enough to name their new
condition something they will recognize
when next we call or next they need to know.

●

Look at the person on your left. Now look
at the one on your right. This time next year
both will be gone. Or this time tomorrow.
History's pecker has eyes. History
can count higher than you, and hold its breath
longer. Look at the smile framed on your desk,
the ones in your wallet. History rolls
like the slow motion film of a fall. With
nothing to grasp, our arms describe perfect
circles; our arc to earth, beauty itself.

●

In a moment everything is altered.
The world spins from a thread tied to the leg
of a hovering sparrowhawk, whose wings
conduct a choir of invisible stars.
Field mice freeze in worship while cold stars sing.
At this altar, everything has moment.
Here, now, the falcon is the one true god.
Her name is Lightness. The world's name is Weight.
Swings the pendulum, frays the thin thread, falls
one feather. This moment is everything.

●

Trapped in the meshes of this neural net,
this translucent tissue, so many small
evanescences: voices, butterflies,
bells, assuming shape, a body the gauze
knows by heart. And recites, neck to navel,
nipple to knee. Light shone through thought shows bells
and butterflies clinging, their bright talc wings
sand mandalas tapped out by bent buddhists,
flour-fine voices of past lovers cooing
like doves huddled on a wire in the rain.

•

I love the world, as does any dancer,
with the tips of my toes. I love the world
more than I love my wife, for it contains
more crannies and crevasses, it tenders
more textures to my twenty digits' touch.
Lush grass underfoot after April rain,
a pile of petals fallen from a rose,
sun-seared sidewalk in summer, sand, fresh-turned
garden dirt, and, yes, her hummocked ankle
rubbed by the ball of my foot as she sleeps.

•

My wife flames in all the colors of gems,
glows glossy as polished igneous rock,
flares like phosphorus. Her lips and hands melt
my misshapen face to pink lava flow.
My wife's fingers flash like the welder's flux,
her feet spark the same blue high c wheels sing
when subway cars take sharp turns. My wife burns
herself into me like specks of iron
ground in red showers from sawn steel. The scars
she leaves deform me but they make me hers.

•

I have seen her assume the shapes of trees,
mountains, calling loons; seen her disappear
into a glacial lake when I canoe
too close; seen ospreys rise from her, and storms;
seen her glistening neck rise from the lake.
I have heard her speak the language of fire,
flowers, and sleepless nights, nights when the sky
explodes into fire and flowers, when sleep
flowers into the language of burning,
one of the languages I learned from her.

·

What every wife should know about her
husband's penis: it does not even need
itself. It prays alone to the Alone.
Like fire, this last limit of the body
ascends in pursuit of what it is not:
idea. You. Think of it as a soul.
Think of it as possessed by lust for truth,
which it seeks in the salt of origin,
as having found the one in the nowhere,
fulfilling its need to become nothing.

·

By all accounts accountable to none,
fascinated with myself, with any
hollow place or prehensile appendage,
I am the leveraged buyout of reason,
the tail that wags the dog, the cat that ate
the coal-black canary, the kid who can't
count and doesn't want to learn, the dark car
passing slowly, twice, in front of your house,
I am the citizen penis, the boys
approaching you on a dark street, laughing.

·

Having fallen so far so suddenly
to so deep darkness, the first last darkness
and the only, only you can end so
long exile, so celestial distance.
So stepfather consoles stepdaughter. So
cold a hand, he says, as mine could be drawn
only to so hot a flame as yours. We
both surrendered. I didn't know the moon
came in so many colors, or said no
as quietly and as often as snow.

·

Are love and rage one passion? Here, frozen
in the hell of violent sensations,
questions burn like ice. Is there a god? *No.*
Was there once a god? *No.* Will god crush you
as he crushed your father and your father's
father? *Yes.* With secret pleasure? *No, with
plainly visible pleasure. The pleasure
birds take out on berries, children on bugs,
bears on salmon, lovers on each other.*
Are love and rage the same? In me? *Hell. Yes.*

·

Sinister shade, source, soul, shared silhouette,
sun-severe singer of curses, singer
of tears, father, don't you see I'm burning?
Don't you see the fallen candle, the sheets
in flames, my singed arm, the others sleeping?
Don't you see the others sleep when you do?
Don't you see I can't? See, I had to die
before you would listen. I had to clutch
the kerosene for this protest, and tug
your sleeve with the same hand that struck the match.

·

From frozen tarn to marmots's cries to moose
everything said *mountain mountain mountain*
in the sun-silvered morse of my own breath.
Everything said I'll breathe before my death
the very days he breathed before my birth.
Loud the sky sounds from inside. The sky shouts
the boy he played baseball with after work
plays ball with someone else's boy today.
No spent life wholly lost, no frost not now
another's cold breath. The clouds said I could climb.

·

Time is the way cold weather and darkness
expand in a mercator projection.
Time is how the organic resists soul.
Time is how the body misbehaves. Time
is the pattern printed on the bedsheets
and how cotton thins and its colors fade.
Time is a boy who can't name his sister
but who can identify prime numbers,
solve long division problems in his head,
and state square roots to seven decimals.

·

Hope names its own absence, a galaxy
older than the universe, *god* the death
of death, water that does not eat light, light
that does not drink water. That means *grief*
names gratitude. For the sound of aspens,
for the chimney's shadow across bright bricks,
for the color of clouds in evening light.
Gratitude that sometimes the body goes
first, that some lives leave a taste like honey
in the rock, some deaths bid the hungry eat.

·

I still cry in places, but not the ones
you would expect. Usually my knees.
Their long, muted wail leaves a trail of ash
in these bones it burrows through to my ears.
Less often in the muscles of my back.
Not that they feel your absence less, only
the dog team waits out the heaviest snows:
they pace and howl, but finally they sleep.
Seldom, thank god, in my forehead, which cries
silently, oblivious to the rain.

•

Then, when facing the future must have seemed
like staring west past a steering wheel at
I-80 leaving Lincoln, you could be
nothing but numb. But don't you feel grief *now?*
Now that happiness has reasserted
itself in her absence, now that moulted
markings have been rendered in fresh feathers?
Isn't it now that sorrow shows itself
for what it is: the ease with which wounds heal,
and that in her absence you remain whole?

•

Behind your kneecaps. In your left femur.
Radiating through your pelvis, lodging
between lumbar vertebrae. In your teeth.
You can feel grief even there, in your teeth.
It scalds your tongue and throat like hot coffee.
It spreads through you, confident as cancer.
Nothing is so delicious. Nothing feels
more like a bird trapped inside your body,
crashing into walls and windows over
and over while the cruel light pours in.

•

Does this site-specific storm system make
me a woman, this ovarian cyst
swelling so close to my soul? Must I die
as a woman to have lived as one? Here,
take these feet of sewn seaweed, this brown mask
braided from corn husks. Bury them with me.
Earth wants herself back, and I will oblige.
This core sample, one inch for each of my
forty-three years, shows the colors of soil
I've become. Earth is a woman I know.

•

If I look down long enough my life looks
like the sky. Crows' tracks registered in mud
reiterate the flocks of geese that cross
my body twice a year crying *Die, die*
horizon to horizon. Looking up
I become the earth: prairies giving birth
to birds that rise in chorus, a single
vulnerability, and then return
like breath. We forgot the land and called it
flight. Now only a fall could recall us.

•

When Thales learned to measure in his head
the surface of earth became a ledger.
The annual Nile flood that gave us mud
gave us maps, calendars imposed on space,
the tablature of number's song. If light
does not seep through a surface, water will.
Burned skin rises, buried bones find the sea.
Pass through one portal into another.
Drive the square-mile county roads in Kansas.
Count the soft woven squares that conceal us.

•

Once a couple of lovers. A couple
of cold friends now. How impotent the hand,
how infinitesimal the abyss
fingertip to fingertip when we stretch,
you prone across the ice, me the scared kid
who fell through. Close enough they would have sparked
once. Close enough to attract iron filings
formed after our former affinity.
Every couple repeats the history
of tangents that once touched but touch no more.

•

The thirty-third time I heard it, your name
became the blaze that cleared the parched prairie,
the fire that opened cones under old growth.
Nothing nurtures like repetition,
or so exposes us as sagittal
sections arranged in rows. No thing repeats,
but all proportions do. Powers of ten,
atom to galaxy. You are to me
as fire to canvas, as tree ring to earth,
as number to a subjugated god.

•

So much for angles and fractions and maps.
It remains now to speak of curvature.
Ice-bent birch branch. Spruce soundboard. Marble hips.
What walks on Euclid in the morning, Gauss
at noon, and Marilyn in the evening?
Never smile at strangers. Never carry
someone else's bags on board. Wait for me.
A streetlamp's halo in a mist at night.
Light from one star bent around another,
masking planets only numbers can see.

•

Grant me a very crude notion of truth:
say six of the sages are guitar strings,
say the seventh files five long fingernails,
say Granados is god. Grant me that truth
imitates fog-muted church bells, soft rain,
thrush's song, that under the stars it sounds
like the stars, like the moon-silhouetted
nighthawks and swifts skittering for insects.
Reason resides in resonant rosewood.
Grant me that. Grant me that strings cannot lie.

•

I confess I have failed you as the sun
in the far northern fall fails finally
and glows a slowly deeper, fainter blue
through leaning megaliths of quiet ice.
I confess I have secrets I still keep
the way a snowscape hides a polar bear.
I confess I am wicked as winter
is dark, cruel as frostbite. Long orphaned
as a child of god, I still have six sides,
and no one of me matches another.

•

In the new world what rolls off whale's flukes
before they sink in slow slow-mo like lives
that flaunt their long leaf-inevitable
leaving will be your song to sift, will sing
through you the way thunder and rough light sing
when waves overwhelm precarious rocks.
There the stars I see through black trees will swarm
to your shoulder while you watch the old earth.
In it your life will glint silver as breath.
I owe you a world, and I plan to pay.

•

I make it my principle to watch you
undress. When you bend for a sock, I count
your vertebrae. I know your underwear
from ten feet, I have pet names for each pair:
Lucky, Climber, Omigod. I make it
my principle to be first in bed, last
to close my eyes. I count your breaths. Some nights
I reach a thousand before I can stop.
If I could die watching you, I would make
it my principle to shorten my life.

•

If bodies are clothes, they should be removed.
Sung, if they are songs. If cats, stroked and stroked.
But if bodies are bodies, already
they cling and purr and sing. Almost without
our help they come unbuttoned and drop down
to ankles that are nearly ours. Without
our hearing them or knowing where they were,
they rub against us, eyes closed, backs arched. If
bodies are bodies, they curl in our laps
and their quiet, half-growled *mmmm* is music.

•

Songs surround us, but we hardly hear them.
Laughing girls speak in rapid Japanese.
The neighbor's sprinkler fortes for the part
of its arc that frets the climbing rose. Crows
bicker. One woman practices her scales,
a cappella. Another sobs. Windchimes
domino the direction of each gust.
A broom rasps across warped, weathered porch boards.
I did it, Mama, a child says. Songs fall
on us as feathers fall on a river.

•

Centaurea cyanus, commonly
called cornflower, once bachelor's button,
croons blue in Finno-Ugric caroming
pine to pine, carols blue in Germanic
careening over the plains. Cornflower
cannot be confined, and knows no revenge,
only travel, only bloom, only blue.
No republic holds it, no soviet,
no reich. Blue speaks a universal tongue.
Indigenous to Europe. Escaped. Free.

•

God being gone, love having left, our sole
remaining task is to define complex
numbers. We know they follow daffodil
but anticipate iris and dogwood.
Early blossoms up, final flurries down
figure the square root of negative one.
Something other than integer squeezes
color from frost. Only complex numbers
can tell how far we need-based petals fall,
our very buds beginning our descent.

•

Cat with no collar, spaniel at Sonic,
a man with green suspenders on the plane.
The gods judge us by how we handle strays.
How many ticks can one coffee can hold?
Experiments in the ruins of math,
we run together like days, like numbers
for checkout boys who can't count back our change,
notes for untrained fingers on untuned strings.
One-and two-and three-and...More coffee grounds
left in the cup than days in our blurred lives.

•

Let me start over. Not so I can speak
clearly, but so I can mimic the gods.
When they command the wind the wind obeys
its own will. I understand the devil's
one melodious truth but not the gods'
polyphonic paradox. Not so I
can say something else, but so I can mean
more by the same thing, more than I meant then,
more than I can know I mean now. More than
the gods, who understand all but themselves.

·

The rules: Make your own lane. Make eye contact
only with equals. Yield to oncoming
traffic. Walk faster than any footsteps
following you. If the Manual wreaks
havoc in the bed, throw it out. Alone
means lost, as does dark. Looking out, not up,
doubles the rent. God sits on the left side
of the plane flying in, and so should you.
Speak seldom, and in another language.
This skyline alone remains of the soul.

·

Here where trees grow up to the street, we need
every possible manner of prayer:
the toddler stopped at the top of the slide,
the open guitar case, the extra coin
in the meter. The glance through the peephole,
the window box planted with white pansies.
We stay on our knees and no longer speak.
We need bike helmet, shoulder belt, sunscreen,
used paperback on the subway. We pray
with sunglasses, house sitters, mace. Hear us.

·

Airfield first, harbor later. My discharge,
due the next day, was delayed by a month,
then brought at last by mortar shell. Certain
Japanese magicians, known to the west
now as legend, could make fall back to earth
alive and completely reassembled
a child they had cut to pieces. The one
I watched passed close enough, strafing the dorm
where I stood watch, for me to see his eyes.
I have seen in this life no child made whole.

·

Liters in hand, wind-bent eyot lives leave
before fish-filled styrofoam flats replace
the milk in the mailboat's hold. Not a tree
limns this archipelago. Human blood,
salty as this sea, here grows just as cold.
Here, what is not rock or water is wind.
Death is wind, and regret, and loneliness.
Without regret, no cure. No fish, no milk.
Brown-and-white boats rock in the mailboat's wake.
On the dock stands a blond girl named Regret.

·

She was wild veronica until she
discovered the lure of iris and rose
and lily-of-the-valley. Any grave
would want to wear her, festooned with her friends.
As a child veronica discovered
herself stemming in curls, swirled like a cape,
unfolding holding her friends' fern-frond hands.
Before she felt the lure of shady beds
and their loose humus, mild veronica
was grave. Until she discovered herself.

·

Leave the package at the door. I will be
tied up. I suck at the Great Mother's breasts,
tipple Tetons, enjoy her Jane Mansfields.
If I ask nicely, she shows me a mean
sunset. I ask nicely. I fondle her
flora and fauna for as long as she
lets me. She lets me as long as I want.
Goddess, she's good, Grand Canyon to K2.
She nudges me to nibble everything
edible, and nearly everything is.

•

A master plaster caster I know made
molds of both his pricks. Prize peckers, I'm told
by one who knows. Well hung, the molds serve her
as tintinnabula, but torment him.
It's nearly impossible to appease
two penises at once. I try to please
both of mine. Tried. I tried taking tinfoil
casts to compare, so they could see themselves
as others do. Other. Significant.
Who can soar without my wings or bells.

•

I imagine whole *species* multiplied
by my sense organ, Sam. Whole worlds, if Sam
had his way. Sam is not a sensible
organ. Seldom does Sam listen to me,
though he holds my attention. Sam's sixth sense
pricks my other five. Sam has a fetish
for certain shapes and colors, certain smells,
certain ways of moving and forms of speech.
Sam has as many fetishes as I.
I make Sam obey. He makes himself heard.

•

Hell's teeth, you're right. We should have. Hell's mouthwash.
By your wife's plump farts and infrequent lusts,
by my half-husband's half-hearted humping,
you're right. Hell's cold sores. Hell's discolored tongue.
If only to prove our first passions wrong,
if only to fail where we could well fail
instead of where we had failed already,
we should have. By her dimpled thighs and his
pimpled ass and our poor judgment, you're right.
Hell's breath. Hell's hot, wholly intent kisses.

•

Do you rejoice at your sister's pleasure,
really? Are you truly happy for her
when she is so much herself she forgets
the difference between man and woman,
finger and tongue, dick and machine? Do you
want to hug her because she feels she is
the ocean, because her salt water flows
without her will, because she bites her lip
so hard it bleeds? Do you worship with her
lover at All Holes Church? Do you believe?

•

Men kneel when she offers the fruits of her
experience: both breasts, all four nipples.
Everything she knows shows in infrared,
including the spectres surrounding her,
not dead enough to be happy, barely
alive enough to be free. Tenebrous,
half in hell, fully in love with licking,
too far from her lignite to flame. Men kneel
when they see so many outlines to trace.
They fade from one earth into another.

•

Lord let my lover be no less laissez
than she is fair, engender her, Jesus,
so she wants out of her jeans as often
as I want in them, make her generous
as algebra, who gives more than is asked
of her, who surprises petitioners
with unexpected solutions to cold
nights and thunderstorms, knows y and y naught,
likes the spot x marks (lingers over it),
kneads perfect numbers from bellies and knees.

●

I would take my lovers, had I any,
to my studio, had I one, to drink
Jack Daniel's or Wild Turkey, whichever
looked more like that day's sun, if the sun shone,
and remind them of parts of themselves they
had forgotten, if I could not work, or
because I cannot work and no longer
want to, since the body's judgment betters
the mind's and it takes lovers to forget
suns, and suns whiskey, and whiskey myself.

●

Men are not required to collaborate
in dreams. A clone in mine begged to borrow
my briefs. Marriage, men, grows flowers and heat.
This is not an institution designed
for a few. Here the masses burrow in
briefly, to nibble on flowers and hide
from the heat. When she wakes to a burro
in my underwear, will she be required
to love that ass no less than she loves mine?
Marriage makes mean dreams. Men are not required.

●

24

A black face surrounded by a bright light.
A beautiful sea-green dress in the place
her scarlet bodice had been. Her double,
the figure of her well-favored figure,
in complementary colors, as if
she had not turned away. Always
I watched from some distance, always she stood
in half shadow. Not quite her, not quite here,
she floats between the white wall and my mind,
there where she is not, her black hair white hot.

•

How could I taste her lips and not my own?
How could I feel her thigh around my thigh
but not mine around hers? How could I smell
her hair but not my nose, feel her rough felt
and inferno but not feel my finger,
and taste the sweet dew morning envies her
but not taste my own tongue? How disappear
so wholly into her without naming
the cries my very spine hears as only
from her, without feeling my breathing stop?

•

A man holds out his hands who wants to know.
How to sate her hungers, and how his own.
Which bulbs to plant in fall, which to dig up.
How to tell the children their dog has died.
Whether to bury it in the yard. How
to have an orgasm with no later
ill effects. Whether he would feel better,
forgiven one of the twelve steps and one
commandment. Why he dreams so frequently
of mountains now, so seldom of the sea.

•

He fondles women, but does not really
rape them. Our irises grew late this spring;
the redbud barely bloomed. Any breeze helps
on a day this hot. I did see someone
suspicious on the street today. I hope
hummingbirds will find our cannas this year.
When she had not returned an hour later,
I went out searching. Songs are hard enough;
maybe prose is impossible. How can
lace this thin let in so little sunlight?

●

Timid flakes like birds' ghosts peck the window,
wanting in. Stay and starve, migrate and die.
What song is there but *Feed me?* Maple leaves
lilt to oblivion. In the garden
one last rosebud opens to this first snow.
Birds' ghosts feed the division of labor
in the sexual act. Snow imitates
maple leaves: migrate and die. When the earth
sings *Feed me,* we join the round. One rosebud
hungers for snow. One leaf labors to earth.

●

No red so gold, no orange so bloody,
no roan so brashly ablaze as the one
that flocked each fall to one now-felled maple.
That color's migration from a solstice
apprenticed to puffins' beaks, wildflowers,
and the midnight sun ended one autumn
at a building not its tree. One autumn
I will build a home for homeless colors.
It will look like the lives that once bore them,
and sound like a grosbeak in the first snow.

●

Call the cliff-face reason while the clips hold,
the ice-sheet truth till it cracks. Call the wind
revelation, the rapids melody.
Still the wisest god could compose no song
more canorous than those our foolish tongues
croon while we drown, those our fingers figure
while we fall. Forgive my frequent missives,
friend, but each inflection may be final,
so I sing not to the infinite but
to you whose fated failure matches mine.

•

After October snow overburdens
the trees and bends their branches to the ground
or the breaking point, whichever comes first.
After stars replace the branches' neck-sharp
snapping with their imitation of grace.
God is for later. After the same snow
that pulled down power lines melts into flood
and spills across thresholds into dark rooms.
After the next front affords frost that blasts
the rose and prints white fossil ferns on panes.

•

Daguerreotype muffled under silver
velvet. Gilt majuscules suffocating
in incunabula. I seldom hear
angels call from the clouds, though
the pawn-sized posturing of pennyworths
I know says I should. The gods gave me up
long ago, so I lift thick flock fabric
from tintypes in dim rooms, rub my fingers
down embossed spines, and pray to dead angels
who made revelation when given none.

•

My first cup of conviction made me retch.
My last cup of courage taught me to count.
The best truths numbers tell end at zero,
as do their best lies. Water knows the one
direction it needs. Light, how to stay warm.
In whose arms, at whose hands, on whose pillow.
At the end of my row give me water
and light and numbers that end in zero
and a name for the color clouds will be
just when I look up, but never again.

•

A little oatmeal lotion to relieve
the itch, a little morphine for the pain.
The toxins told her all she had to know.
No more dialysis, she said one day,
adding *no more rain* to *the no more snow*
she did not choose. Her daughters bathed her, one
her legs, one her face, one their origin.
She weary, sister. Doan git so wary.
Eyes open in her final sleep, she said
I see God! What does he say? *Nothing yet.*

•

God he spoke and then the chariot stop.
Never mind she was forty-six and he
was fifty-two. The eighteen-wheeler spoke.
Never mind this was her first best marriage
and she was a virgin. Never mind they
had just left the church. The chariot stop.
Never mind it was dragged a quarter mile.
The sparks they sang. The driver he saw God
bearing down, but he saw one breath too late.
"God!" he spoke. But then the chariot stop.

•

Only after the drifts covered the car
did I know I would die there. Snow stores light.
Even under a twelve-foot drift, at night,
in a storm, after the frostbite has reached
your ankles, snow *glows*. Dimly, but it glows,
loaded with bright angels that floated down,
jellyfish adrift in a cold black sea.
I gave in to sleep, already chalk, white
under layers of lives that will rise up
in ten million years to glint in the sun.

·

Señoritas mummied in Juarez sun,
pants around their ankles, beetle holes bored
in black cheeks, blank eyes. Pakistani boys
bent over looms. Did I fail to mention
the price of light? What looks like luxury
is. God's compound eye, we witness the world,
his body, burned by the halogen bulb.
Fire in the east, fire in the west. Plenty
to trust the truth, plenty to deny it,
and none but lucifer to know better.

·

The hawk enfolded in the fist fights song
by crying a warning. Seven white hares
huddle in the held breath. The body's speech
is our only speech, its hush all we know
of silence. Even when we overhear
the rain, we need translation into touch.
Nothing speaks like bone stridulating bone.
Nothing ciphers like fingertip to wrist,
the clicks and hums of whale calling to whale
in language older than the sea is vast.

·

Next to my favorite room in the world
(a screened porch with space for the two of us,
our rocking chairs, and as end tables slabs
of rough-cut elm balanced on old cream cans)
I've planted angels, wild perennials
that call across mountains and parallels
to hummingbirds and through old growth to bees.
He and I live a pestilence and die
a meteor but my sweet profligate
cherubs scent days too furious, too few.

•

How do you like paradise so far? Stay.
Its charm burns off like morning rain. Crabs clean
these rocks by hand. You will regret feelings
so exquisite. Earth screamed our birth with fire:
the end will come when the sea loses count.
One god named the old island, another
will name the new. Teach me to lay my eggs
in sand, I'll teach you to breathe in the sea.
Watch for the silhouetted shearwater
at sunset zipping the horizon closed.

•

Rocks risen from rocks, rounded by roiling.
Clattering leaves on the coconut palms.
Clouds colored by contact: sea-dark below,
sun-bright above. For everything you know
but will not tell, something else surrounds you
without your knowledge. Smaller than nipples,
a million snails climbing the wet seawall.
Their ancestors disguised as sand teaching
crabs color, their sisters trapped in tidepools.
The soft, soft song of the susurrate surf.

•

What you call courage floats in the cold sea
longer than do we who shiver, then sink
out of sight of the sun. What you call love
I carved into a birch box I set out
at night with food for the new ghost, the one
who calls you Courage and names me Nothing,
though my face is his. Who will not set foot
on the porch if I am watching but floats
in the dark night longer than it takes me
to see my own face in yours while you sleep.

●

Soften the mountain for centuries, then
swallow the city in minutes. Ships sink
near shore. The sea is the richest nation
after the soil. Two coins in every grave,
no eyes. The medulla oblongata
is a lovely and serious object.
Swallow the ant in seconds, but save it
for centuries. Bury sons in the sea,
daughters in soil. Two pennies for your thoughts.
We must be safe here, so far from the shore.

●

The negation of a relation is
a relation. I name our negation
Nereus for the father I am not,
no matter our daughters' needs, no matter
my own. Nereus names how transient I
must be in their element, they in mine,
how unlike are water and air. When you
negated me, my relation to them
turned orphan to orphan, but Nereus
none of us can negate, no matter what.

●

I name myself Rosalind whenever
he beats me, because so little blood needs
emphasis, some red to balance the blue
of bruises that darken me as dampness
darkens dishrags. Because the bruises bloom
the way buds bloom: delicately, briefly.
To understand my mind, you would need to
understand my body the way he does,
as a sea turtle understands the earth
and wants to cry out to it but cannot.

•

An accurate self-portrait would not look
like me. Black bile and spit in a small vial—
there. Truth is hard to swallow. Pubic hair
bound in a bow. Shall I enumerate
my humors? Blood, bile, choler, come. Come, come:
how many more lies must I tell, how much
closer must I stand before you see me?
I thought of eating a gun, but this death
seemed more revealing. My life. I call it
Self-Portrait in Shit and Underarm Hair.

•

My friends glimpse ghosts in stairwells and hear them
padding past office doors at night. My friends
wear gold rings given them by aliens.
They see Elvis. They talk to God. Why not,
when I have never doubted you loved me?
Why do we *believe* anything at all?
Why do I still hide the gold ring the sun
gave me? Why does your ghost take off its shoes
at my office door? Why will it not speak
in any voice except the voice of God?

•

Flutes, bells, human voices. Spring. Lawnmower
in thick grass, almost stopped, catching its breath.
The grating of a plumber's snake scraped up
and down the neighbor's gutters. Bells, voices,
the calls of cardinals, trimmer whining
through wet grass, a dog jogging by, panting
with its master, the reeling of its leash
when it stops. I don't believe in gods, but
I believe in signs. The clack of roller-
blades across cracks in the sidewalk. Flutes. Bells.

·

Voices of geese in the yellow night sky.
If it meant something other than itself
their song would sound less like God. If they meant
something less than God, the geese would not sing.
Over me music, under me water.
One family portrait per funeral.
Each year the geese name one more missing face.
Each season the hazed light that hides their flight
mutes their song. And the mist that soaks sidewalks
and stains roofs glints on cars under streetlights.

·

We have come in your dreams, a hundred eyes
atop the fence then moving toward you
through the dark yard like approaching planets,
to fulfill your own predictions. We've come
to tell you our names, which are unlike yours.
We've come to leave urgent, inscrutable
messages, on which your life and the lives
of your children depend, to satisfy
an appetite you have misnamed *spirit,*
our name for which you cannot understand.

·

In case of police, I keep at all times
an emergency packet: a toothbrush,
toothpaste, a razor, soap, some underwear,
a good book, a pen and paper, one leaf,
an etui with a lock of my wife's hair.
In case of the gods, I carry with me
the Estonian word that names winter,
a tune Brouwer calls "Berceuse," the six months
Alma Ettie saved for her daughter's trike,
the smell of lilac and mint after rain.

·

My joints make noises when I kneel beside
the flowers. Nowadays my joints demand
always to be heard. I need a stick now
to stand back up. I teeter between rows
of tomatoes, where soon a fall will break
a hip. My fingers no longer straighten,
nor does my back. I ask not to transcend
this body but to reclaim it. Not that
my husband's mind be right again, but that
he stop crying. I see nothing, clearly.

·

Friends feel pain not at corresponding spots
but in the *same* place. Call it God, call it
the heart, but call it. Winter always feels
unusually cold here where its rules
demand exceptionally long darkness.
Friends feel pain wherever time mislays it,
in an office savaged by Soviet
soldiers, in a sister's lost words, or propped
against the joy I feel when suddenly
I understand how to translate your life.

·

At sea level earth still thinks it can rise,
the lungs still eat solid food. Desyatins
dense with dust, limestone-stained grasses lining
gravel roads, and serried smog-shrouded squares
sediment. Either see the stars or breathe:
no simple choice. I recommend burning
legs, a face blue as night. I recommend
height. Whatever else I do, I'll show you
a mountain where only eyes can inhale,
where everything is ice or light. Or both.

·

A yellow square revealed by scratching off
a black wash, the neighbor's kitchen window
frames an eggshell blue vase and her housecoat
the color of clover. A violent violet
sprayed across the sky presages thunder.
Through strict obedience to light, color
enjoys considerable liberty:
next day the same blue will spread horizon
to horizon the fragrance Ariel
inhaled in the new and limitless world.

·

Cormorant perched atop a rocking mast.
Gull wheeling, then plunging into the sea.
Puffin staring across waves, a widow.
I speak here of angels, but I mean men.
Puffin flapping faster than angels' words.
Gull in wind flying backward, a devil.
Cormorant rocking, spread wings praising light.
Here, waves speak to men often of angels.
Widowed angels speak seldom of the sea.
Men tied to masts see angels in the wind.

·

The god of mathematics must have felt
this frustration when he fractaled feathers
enough for the first flight, then watched from earth.
I have serried here every syllable,
numbered everything I know and then some,
but still late snow blackens these bare branches
as it melts to mud, still skeletal dogs
stare from roadsides, already my digits
number my days with painful rigidity.
I have not said what I wanted to say.

FIGURES

Everything now depended on him. He could make
the right gesture, or the wrong one, but he could
not know beforehand which was which.
Experience had taught him that reason
could not be counted on in such
situations. There was always an
extra element, mysterious and not quite within reach, that one had not
reckoned with. One had to know, not deduce. And he did not have the
knowledge.

I was actually hearing it *make no sense.*

I try to channel my pain in a single direction,
to aim it at something moving away from me.
If I can make my pain one kind of pain
instead of three or seven it becomes less painful.
When I cannot channel my pain, when they win,
I cannot scream because they will not let me breathe,
and I cannot kill myself because they bind my hands.
They travel together. They circle me, barking.
They hunt at night when only their eyes are visible.
They make the stars. They are the stars.
I name them because I know they name each other.
They call to each other across me. They speak in code.
They tell each other all my weaknesses. They laugh.
I can hear them stalking me. I know which ones
are hunting me before they know I am their prey.
I know their habits, when they feed and how they travel,
but nothing helps except to make them one, so I picture them
single file, eyeing me as they back out of my head
through a distant hole visible as a pinpoint of light.

●

Do you sometimes lie when it would be easier to tell the truth?
    No, of course not. How could I? Nothing could be easier than lying.
Do you ever catch others in lies they have not yet told?
    I prefer freedom to truth. I don't let what I mean limit what I say.
Do you lie to yourself without knowing it? Would you tell me if you did?
    In fact, I never let what I mean limit anything I do.
I trust you because you always lie to yourself before you lie to me.
    Why should I live in only one world when I can live in many?
If you will tell me something I already know, I will believe you.
    Why should I be one person when I can surprise myself?
I trust you because you contradict yourself in interesting ways.
    You trust me not because I tell the truth, but because you do.

●

I have relationship problems. I'm sorry. It's not your fault.
You could have been anyone. It would have ended this way
no matter who you were. Nothing has changed, really.
Nothing about you now is any different than before.
Attraction plays by its own rules. No single feature is yours alone:
plenty of people have your eyes or your voice or your smile.
Why the combination of perfectly common features
that makes you you attracted me I do not know, or why
that combination now repels me. Please do not take this personally.
In some games the rules change while we play. This has happened before.
You knew when we started you were not the first. You had to know.
No one is ever the first. Not even the first is the first.
Whatever happened with the first already happened before.
Did you think you would be an exception? It would not matter
what you were like, or what you did, or how you treated me.
You treat me just fine. Only you no longer attract me,
probably because you are not my father. No one is,
anymore. In fact, no one ever was. Certainly not him.
He was always doing things he was not supposed to do,
with people he was not supposed to do them with,
especially me. Then he died, which he was not supposed to do
either, not then anyway, before I could tell him I knew
the whole time he was doing them that he should not have been doing
the things he did with me. Now what am I supposed to do,
and with whom? You see the problem. I am attracted
only when I should not be, to people who should not attract me,
so that now when the consummation of our mutual attraction means
I should continue being attracted to you, that same consummation
means I cannot. My attraction to you could have lasted
only if you had not been attracted to me. I wish
I could have spared you, but I did not know this myself,
or rather the way in which I knew it was not helpful.
I hope this is not too sudden. I would have warned you
had I myself been warned. I will not trouble you for long.
In fact I will be gone the rest of the time I am here.

•

I don't think you understand me.
My grief as a girl over my father's frequent absences
matched my fear of his return.
He taught me never to tell.
My mother taught me never to ask.
   I don't think you understand me.
A man's voice carries farther before sundown,
a woman's after. A man's voice carries farther
through air, a woman's through water.
   I don't think you understand me.
The few prisoners who survived dismemberment
were forced to eat each other's limbs.
   I don't think you understand.

•

We regret to inform you that what we have to say
is something you will not want to hear.
We assure you that we did not want to say it,
and that in saying it we mean well.
Please understand that what we have to say
does not reflect on you or on us or on anything
except the regrettable circumstances which dictate
our saying it. We hope it will help to know
that we have had to say the same thing to others,
though we would rather have said to them then
what circumstances preclude our saying to you now.
We hope that soon someone will say to you
what we wish we could say but cannot,
and that you will continue to view us
in the same favorable light as before we were forced
to say what we must.

•

I thought you would tell me if something was wrong.
   I thought you would ask me if you wanted to know.
When there were problems before, you always told me.
   When I told you things before, you never listened.

When things went wrong, you could count on my being there.
When you were there, I could count on things going wrong.
You should have asked me to leave if I caused such problems.
You should have left without having to be asked.
I never did anything without first thinking of your happiness.
You never did anything without thinking you were my happiness.
Nothing can take away what we had together.
We had nothing together that you have not already taken away.

•

I have tired of making sense. I make sense all the time. Everyone says so,
even you, in your own way, though you never come out and say it,
since you never come out and say anything. Not anything you mean.
Mother used to tell me I made sense. That seemed to matter at the time,
the way it matters now when you tell me. The kind of mattering that tells
    me
I have not done what is expected of me, that what is expected of me is
    impossible,
and that it is my job to discover what is expected because no one will tell
    me.
Though I am still obliged to do it, even if I cannot find out what it is.
Father never told me I made sense, but his was the kind of not telling
that meant not to say everything it did not say, not the kind of not telling
like yours and mother's that means to say what it does not.
Who am I making sense to? No one makes sense to me. Even I,
for all my making sense to others, make precious little sense to myself.
Though, unlike everyone else, I try, very hard. But now
I am through with that, the trying to make sense.
This will make sense later, if it ever makes sense.
It would make more sense if you were me.
A lot of things would make more sense, to me at least,
if you were me, or if at least I were someone else. As in fact I am.
You have always been me more than I have been me.
Unlike me, you always knew what you wanted me to be,
and why I was not what you wanted, and what I could do to change.
Unlike me, you always knew what I meant to say.
You always read in my face glyphs I did not write there
and could not believe when you read them to me.

I know now that making sense only attracts the wrong kind of people.
The kind who want to be things with names, and want to have things
that can be had, the kind who are forever wanting things explained,
the kind who refuse explanations, who because they cannot make sense
envy sense in others, crave it for themselves, track it, spy on it, enforce it.
I do not want to be with anyone I could attract, including you,
whom I once attracted, and still attract in the attenuated sense
in which attraction can be perpetuated. We made sense together,
which is what attraction is, or was with us at least.
When I moved, you moved. My foot always landed
where yours had just been. But flashes of insight are brief.
If they lasted, so would we. Nothing would change.
Everything would go on just as long as it made sense to continue.

•

I don't think I love you like I used to.
After he had tightened the knot on his tie
and shrugged his jacket back on,
after he had opened the door,
he said he would not be back.
I don't think I love you like I used to.
A planet strays from orbit,
a human child is born blind.
A star explodes into color invisible to our eyes.
I don't think I love you like I used to.
Wind longs for heaven, leaves long for earth:
their courtship is exciting but brief.
I don't think I love you.

•

How did you know what I should feel before I knew I should feel it?
I would more readily believe I should feel what you say I should feel
if you didn't say I should feel it. I would pretend to have the feelings
if I could, to make you happy and so I could believe them myself,
but when I pretend to feel what you say I should feel, it upsets you.
And once you have told me I should feel it I can only pretend that I do,
because to really feel what you say I should feel, I would have to feel it

without being told to. I don't know how it became so important to you
that I feel what I didn't know I was not feeling, or how you came to believe
I was feeling what I couldn't possibly feel, or how to overcome my own
    doubt
that you feel what you say you feel. What you say I should feel
so closely matches what you say you feel that since I myself can't feel it
I also can't believe you really feel it. Or see why it matters.
All this time I thought it was enough that I wanted to make you happy.
All this time I thought I could.

•

I will be late this evening. Go ahead and have supper without me.
    I will not be here when you get home, whenever that is.
I have a lot of things to finish up here, things that have to get done.
    I will leave a note telling you in general terms where I have gone.
There are things to finish up there, too, I know, but these are easier.
    It will be nowhere you have heard of or would ever want to go.
These things, though they come back later, can at least be made to
    disappear.
    I will leave directions, but they will lead somewhere else.
Those things never go away, even for a minute, no matter what I do.
    Somewhere else has always been your favorite place to be.
I feel more comfortable here, where I can sign my name.
    This was your last bad habit. Be proud. I have finally become you.

•

She does not have to love him. No one has to.
No one has to love anyone. She couldn't love him if she had to.
Love just doesn't work that way. It's not like breathing, for god's sake,
though what you want plays the same role in each.
Love is not like anything: if it were, we would know how it works.
Think of what will happen if she doesn't love him.
He will go right on being unlovable just like he would have,
but he will also be unloved, and that will be her fault
because she could love him. If she does love him,
it won't keep him from being unlovable, of course,
but it will make the being unlovable his fault.

Then it will be him losing sleep at night instead of her.
Except that people who are unlovable never believe they are.
It doesn't matter what he's done to her. If she loved him
she wouldn't let that get in the way. That he did what he did to her
proves she is the one who should love him. He could have done it
to anyone. He does it to make up for what he would do
if he were not unlovable. She should learn to like it.

·

I don't think I want to anymore.
For years the dog growled, muzzle through the fence
when the woman wheeled her husband past.
The first day she passed by alone,
the dog watched from the porch.
I don't think I want to anymore.
The same salinity that silts our humors
infuses their sister, the sea.
The same lights swim in each.
I don't think I want to anymore.
A drowned man will not sink
until a woman is drowned.
I don't think I want to.

·

Don't wait on me, she said. Patience is a virtue,
and you should spend your energy
preserving those few virtues you possess
instead of wasting it chasing new ones.
I can catch up. You go on by yourself,
wherever you are going. You have told me
a thousand times where that is, but I keep forgetting,
and there is no point in telling me
while I am concentrating on getting ready
for whatever we are going to do.
It won't start without me, whatever it is.
You go on ahead. I have a few things to finish around here,
but none are important enough to make you wait.

Nothing is important enough to make you wait.
Our going together matters less than your being there.
Your being in such a rush told me that,
and my running late shows I agree.
It is such a long way that you should start now
if you want to be there on time.
Anything could happen along the way.
Something could fall out of the sky.
Something that should work might not.
Something might be in your way.
You should leave yourself time for any contingency,
including the possibility that I will decide
not to go wherever you are going, or to be
where you expect me when you return.

·

Are you now recording, or have you ever recorded, a conversation between
    us?
    I don't recall our ever having had a conversation. I don't believe I know you.
You've been recording everything I say. I've seen you. You want revenge.
    'Recording' is not the word I would use. I prefer the term 'registering.'
If I said 'recording,' what word would you use to affirm or deny?
    In a given context, any number of words may be equally appropriate.
Do you really consider your choice of words a help in this situation?
    No word can help a situation in which the damage is irreparable.
We have to live with each other, you know. Neither of us can go away.
    I seldom see you, even when I look at you. Especially when I look at you.
Of course we can live around each other instead of with each other.
    I haven't seen you now for years. Or only the you I needed to see.
If I am always where you are not, you will always be where I am not.
    In fact I have my doubts that you exist at all, or have existed, or ever will.

·

Once it started the way it started, it had to go the way it went.
Nothing else explains why we did what we did to each other
for so long, so painfully, at such cost, with full knowledge.
I hated what I was doing to you as much as what you were doing to me,
but we couldn't stop, because we had started the way we had.
Each of us was what the other wanted, but once we had what we wanted
there was nothing left for us to want but what we didn't want.
We didn't want it to end this way, so we should have known it had to.

•

I don't think I can tonight.
After daring me to lay my hand on the table,
my five-year-old brother broke my finger with a hammer.
I was four. Neither of us knew how badly one person
can hurt another without meaning to.
I don't think I can tonight.
The corpses of everyone who ever starved to death
would reach to the sun and back,
but would not cover the sea floor.
I don't think I can tonight.
The two arteries that pass beneath the pelvic bone
into the penis are named Misery and Misery.
I don't think I can.

•

I was never in control. My body left me.
I had to tell it what to do, like having to explain a joke
or tell a lover what you want or interpret a dream,
knowing my instructions were no solution,
only infallible proof that something was wrong.
Everything was happening an instant too late,
like sound arriving always just after the flash.
No one warned me this would happen
or told me how to make it stop.
No one gave me any information I could use.
The rescue parties arrived only after I had frozen.
I watched myself do it. I didn't try to stop myself,

since I didn't know what I was doing.
In fact I don't know now what I did,
though I do remember doing it, whatever it was.
I remember what her eyes looked like
the instant I did whatever I did,
and that both of us were scared,
I because I was not in control of myself,
and she because she was not in control of me.
It was not whatever I did that was wrong,
but how and why I did it, and who I did it to.
She knew it was wrong, but she couldn't tell me.
She tried to, but I wouldn't listen. I couldn't.
Her words didn't match the movement of her lips.
She was crying, but it didn't sound like crying
or feel like crying until after she stopped.